Sudden Impact

Lesley Choyce

Orca currents

ORCA BOOK PUBLISHERS

Library and Archives Cataloguing in Publication

Choyce, Lesley, 1951-
Sudden impact / Lesley Choyce.

(Orca currents)
ISBN 1-55143-476-8

I. Title. II. Series.

PS8555.H668S82 2005   jC813'.54   C2005-904074-2

Summary: Tina needs to find an organ donor to save Kurt's life.

First published in the United States, 2005
Library of Congress Control Number: 2005929724

Orca Book Publishers gratefully acknowledges the support for its
publishing programs provided by the following agencies: the Government
of Canada through the Book Publishing Industry Development Program
and the Canada Council for the Arts, and the Province of British Columbia
through the BC Arts Council and the Book Publishing Tax Credit.

Cover design: Lynn O'Rourke
Cover photography: Getty Images

Orca Book Publishers   **Orca Book Publishers**
PO Box 5626, Stn. B   PO Box 468
Victoria, BC Canada   Custer, WA USA
V8R 6S4   98240-0468

www.orcabook.com
Printed and bound in Canada.
Printed on 100% PCW recycled paper.

09 08 07 06 • 5 4 3 2

chapter one

I was excited about seeing the soccer game later, but there was something about the way Kurt was acting at lunch that worried me. He looked pale.

"Are you all right?" I asked.

"I'm fine," he said. He didn't look fine.

"Is there something wrong?" He was staring at his lunch tray, but he wasn't eating.

"I just don't think I can eat another cafeteria meal."

"I know what you mean," I said, but I was sure there was more to Kurt's loss of appetite. "Are you nervous about the game?"

"No way," he said defensively. "I can't wait to play. I've been training for this day all summer."

"But if you're sick..." He didn't let me finish the sentence.

Suddenly he was angry at me. "Hey, what's going on today? First my mom gives me a hard time and says I should stay home from school. Now you start hassling me."

"Sorry," I said. It wasn't like Kurt to be nasty to me. We always got along so well.

I was the reason Kurt made the soccer team—because I like to run. I don't know why I like to run. My mother said I never walked anywhere when I was a little girl. I ran. I was always the first to arrive. It wasn't that I was in a hurry. I just liked the way I felt when I was running. Free and alive.

For a while, Kurt made fun of me. He kept saying I should slow down. And I did. If I wanted to walk to school with Kurt, I had to walk at his pace. It drove me crazy at first, but I learned to do it because I needed him as a friend. I really did.

I had asked Kurt once if there was anything he liked to do as much as I liked running. "When I was younger, I really wanted to be good at something. First it was hockey. Then swimming. But I sucked. I was just never very good at the things I wanted to be good at."

"What about now?" I'd asked.

"I'd like to be good at...something. Soccer, I think. I play with the guys for fun, but I'm not that good. I don't have what it takes."

"I bet you could if you wanted to."

"I'd like to be on the school team more than just about anything in the world."

"Then do it."

"I can't. Tryouts are in three weeks. But it would just be a waste of time."

"We'll train. What are you weakest at?"

He had laughed. "Running," he'd said. "I don't seem to have any endurance. After ten minutes in a game, I'm wasted. It's embarrassing."

"I'll be your trainer," I'd said. "In three weeks you'll be able to run a mile. If you can run a mile, you'll do well in soccer."

"I can't do it. I've tried before. I can't."

"You just never had the right coach," I'd said. "Follow me."

And I started running. Kurt followed.

I taught him to pace himself. I told him about breathing. Sometimes he'd get a cramp and we'd stop. Even then I worried there was something physically wrong with him. Once he felt better we'd run some more. First we ran one block. Then two. Then all the way to the school. Then to the river. Then farther. By the time the tryouts started, Kurt was a runner.

He made the team and was really excited. So was I—at first. But then I was kind of mad at him. Now it was all about soccer. No more running after school with me. Kurt started hanging out with this older guy on the team named Jason. He'd known Jason from way back, but I don't think they'd had much in common before. Now they were both on the team. Jason didn't like me, but I tried not to let it bother me.

Jason could be mean to Kurt too. Jason was sixteen, two years older than Kurt and me, and he had this way of putting people down. In the halls he'd make fun of Kurt for having a girl for a best friend as if there was something wrong with it. I'd just snap back something like, "Why don't you clean the grunge out from under your toenails and eat it for breakfast?" Jason would fake like he was hurt and slink off down the hall.

I think Jason was angry that Kurt played soccer as well as he did, even though Kurt was younger. Kurt and Jason both played halfback. They could both run five miles without getting winded, and they both had legs like lighting when it came to kicking the ball into the net.

But every time Kurt passed the ball because he had three players all over him, Jason was on him like maggots on dead meat. "What's wrong, Kurtie, legs turn to mush again?" Or, "C'mon, dude, you can't wimp out like that." And Jason's theme song on the field, the phrase he said over and over to Kurt was, "You'll never do anything great unless you take a few chances. Go for it, man. Don't always play it safe." Maybe that philosophy worked for Jason.

chapter two

It was the first official game of the year. Memorial was playing Fairview in what was predicted to be one very serious game of soccer. I'd been to practices before to watch Kurt, but this was different.

The Memorial coach was sending the first string out onto the field. Kurt had been playing against Jason up until now—red team against the blue. But this was the real thing.

Two halfbacks were to go out on the field to play, and the coach had already sent out Jason. That meant he had to pick between Kurt and Dennis Rankin, one of his personal favorites. The whistle blew. The field was full except for one halfback slot on our team. Coach Kenner couldn't seem to make up his mind. He was standing there, his bald head gleaming in the sunshine, looking at the annoyed referee and shaking his head. Finally he pointed a finger at Kurt. "Go," he said.

Kurt ran for the field, and the whistle blew. The game began and players were running back and forth like angry animals.

Fairview had the stronger team. They were faster and had better control of the ball. They scored almost as soon as the game began. Jason yelled at Kurt to get the lead out. That's when I noticed that Kurt was holding his side like he had a cramp or something. When the whistle blew again, though, he took off like lightning.

The ball was passed to Kurt and he worked it downfield, his teammates trying to keep up with him. Just as he was about to get crowded out by his opponents, he kicked the ball across the field to Jason. Jason let out a hoot and moved deeper into Fairview territory as Kurt slipped back, slowing down and clutching his side again.

That was the funny thing about Kurt and Jason. At school, they were mortal enemies. Even during practice, Jason gave Kurt a hard time. But once they were on the field together they were like brothers. Jason set Kurt up for a good shot on goal, and then there was Kurt, setting Jason up for what should have been an easy goal.

But something went wrong. Just as Jason was about to kick the ball into the net, a Fairview player sneaked up behind him with a burst of speed and tapped the ball away to one of his own players. In an instant, the ball was headed back down the field, and the whole game shifted.

Jason tripped over the Fairview player's foot and came down hard on the grass, cursing. The trip hadn't been intentional, but Jason had a short fuse. He reached out and grabbed the Fairview player by his jersey and pulled him down. I saw Jason say something nasty to the guy and then jab him with an elbow before rolling over. Jason stood. He looked a bit shaky and limped slightly as he tried to get back into the game.

Kurt was in the center of the action farther up the field but was having no luck getting the ball away from the Fairview player. When the guy made his move, Kurt tried to put himself in the way of the kick, but he was unsteady as he ran and couldn't do anything. Something wasn't right. Maybe it was just nerves, but I could see Kurt wasn't playing his best. I remembered that his mother had tried to talk him out of playing. I was getting worried.

Fairview scored their second goal and got a big roar of approval from the crowd that had come to support them.

Someone called a time-out, and the Fairview player who'd stolen the ball from Jason was now talking to his coach. The Fairview coach called the ref and pretty soon they were walking across to talk to Coach Kenner.

I could see Kenner looked angry, but then he nodded his head. He waved Jason off the field. Jason was in trouble for something he had said to the Fairview player, I guessed. Or that jab to the ribs. Not a nice way to play soccer. Dennis Rankin got the nod and headed out onto the field while Jason sat down to watch the game from the bench. He looked like he was ready to scream.

chapter three

When the game resumed Jason started going nuts on the sidelines. He screamed something at Kurt who now had an odd wobble to the way he was running. I could tell, though, that Kurt was giving it all he had. He seemed to be moving in slow motion, but he wasn't giving up. I didn't like the look on his face, but I didn't know what to do.

Fairview had the ball, yet again, and were only meters from our goal. Kurt tried to slip between two opposing players like a quarter being dropped into a pay phone. He ducked low, got control of the ball and suddenly got his energy back. He raced down the field and made a pass to Wicket. As soon as Wicket was swarming with Fairview defensemen, he returned the ball to Kurt.

I don't think his feet even touched the ground, and he had perfect control of the ball. A fullback and a goalie were all that were in the way. I'd seen Kurt operate with two men on him before. He could turn into a snake and get around guys like there was nothing to it.

I held my breath as he set himself up to make his shot. The ball was off. I tried to follow the ball, but then I heard an awful thud. I turned to see Kurt falling to the ground.

The Fairview fullback had tried to block Kurt's shot. He missed the ball, and his foot came up hard and caught Kurt below the ribs. I grabbed my own sides and felt sympathy pain as Kurt fell to the ground.

The heavy fullback went down right on top of him. I heard this terrifying scream come out of Kurt. Kurt was not usually a screamer. I'd never heard him utter the slightest whimper of pain, ever. He was as tough as they come.

A whistle blew. The ball had missed the net. Nobody knew what I knew. I was over the rickety fence and running onto the field. The referee pulled the Fairview goon off of Kurt, but Kurt was still curled over on the grass.

Coach Kenner yelled at me to get off the field. He and Jason both came chasing after me. They thought I'd lost my mind. *A kid falls down in a soccer game, big deal.* But I knew better.

The ref had his hand on Kurt's shoulder, and the other players had moved back. Kurt was gulping for air and let out a terrible moan like he was trying to cry but couldn't. I put my face close to his and saw that his skin was clammy and pale. I tried to hear what he was saying and could finally make out the words, "Help me."

Coach Kenner pulled me away and was still acting like it was no big deal. Jason, that is to say, the nasty version of Jason, started ranting and raving, "Look at this guy. He takes a fall, gets the wind knocked out of him and acts like he's dying. What a joke."

Maybe Jason thought he could shame his teammate into getting up and back into the game. I gave him a look that would have made any intelligent creature run for cover.

"Call an ambulance," I said, my voice shaking.

The other players all looked at me like I was crazy. Jason played it for all it was worth. "What is this? Kurt has to have a girl come to the rescue every time he falls down? Is this the sort of weakling we want on our team?"

"Call an ambulance," I said louder this time.

No one paid attention. The ref, however, bent over Kurt, pushing me out of his way. He looked up at Kenner. "She's right. Call an ambulance."

chapter four

The coach asked if anyone from the team would volunteer to go with Kurt to the hospital.

"I'll go," I said, but he looked right past me like I didn't matter.

Jason said, "Yeah, let her go. We need our team players here. We've got a game to play." He was still treating this like it was nothing. And it was funny because no one on the team did volunteer. Either they had got a good look at Kurt and were too scared to go along, or they wanted to get back to their game. I don't know which.

"I'm going," I said, looking straight at the coach. "Get out of my way."

The guys from the team just stood there and stared at me. Fortunately there was a woman inside the ambulance, a black woman who took control of the situation. She realized that they weren't going to move unless I was inside. "Get in, honey," she said. "Just sit tight and let us do our work."

I got in. The man driving the ambulance fired up the siren, and we sped off across the soccer field and past the high school. As we went out the driveway, I looked at the brick school building through the back window, and it all looked different. I had a feeling that things would never be quite the same. Kurt was unconscious. His skin looked awful. The ambulance lady put an oxygen mask over his face. She carefully studied Kurt's breathing. She looked up at me and tried to fake a smile. "What's your name?" she asked.

"Tina."

"I'm Martha. You know this guy?"

I tried to talk but couldn't. Nothing came out; I was that scared. Martha seemed to understand right away what Kurt meant to me.

"Hang onto that strap," she said, pointing to a rope loop above me head. I grabbed it. Then she yelled to the driver, "I think this calls for a little more action, Vince."

Vince hit the siren again and punched the gas pedal to the floor. We flew around a corner and I held on to the strap. Martha smiled at me again. It was a warm smile this time. "Vince likes it when he gets to drive fast," she said, pretending that it was all a game—that Kurt wasn't as bad off as I knew he was.

At the hospital, I was pushed out of the way by the two orderlies who helped wheel Kurt into Emergency. Kurt was still unconscious. I wanted to keep asking, *What is it? What's wrong? Will he be okay?* But I had given up. Nobody was going to answer my questions because nobody knew what exactly was wrong with Kurt.

They wheeled Kurt down a long hallway, and I tried to get a good view of which room they took him into. A nurse took me by the sleeve, sat me down and started asking me questions about Kurt. "We have to call his parents," she said. "Do you know the number?"

I gave her Kurt's phone number, and she left to make the call.

I sat down and tried to relax but couldn't. Martha came in and found me sitting on the edge of the chair. "I wish I could hang around and keep you company, Tina, but I've got another call." She handed me some change. "Go get Coke," she said. "Everything will be okay. Things usually aren't as bad as they seem, believe me." She gave my hand a squeeze and then turned to go.

I was in a funny haze, and I almost thought I was going to pass out. I took a deep breath and stumbled up the hallway to the pop machine. I popped the quarters in but stood there looking at the choices. I couldn't think straight. I needed to see Kurt right then and make sure he was alive.

I made a fist and smacked it hard onto the side of the machine, then ran down the long hallway. An orderly grabbed me and said, "You can't go down there," but I pulled away and kept going until I saw a sign over a door that said EMERGENCY.

Inside I saw a little kid crying as he got stitches in his forehead. Nearby an old flabby guy with no shirt on was taking a deep breath while a doctor held a stethoscope to his chest. Then I saw Kurt, stretched out on a hospital bed. He was still unconscious. Two doctors and a nurse were bent over him. They appeared serious and desperately concerned.

The nurse inserted a tube into Kurt's arm as I sidled up. The tube was connected to an elevated bottle of clear liquid. "Is he going to be all right?" I asked her.

"You shouldn't be in here," she said, sounding like a cold-hearted mother disciplining a bad child.

"Is he going to be all right?" I demanded.

The doctors were trying to ignore me. One nodded to the nurse to remove me from the room. She tried to grab onto me, but I shook her off. "I'm staying," I said defiantly. Maybe I was wrong to be so stubborn, but I had a feeling that if I walked out of that room I might never see Kurt again.

One of the doctors, a young guy with glasses, turned to me. He acted like this was no big deal, like it happened all the time. In a cool, clinical voice, he said, "I'm Dr. Bennington. Could you describe the accident please?"

I told him what I had seen and he nodded. "Was he all right before the game?"

I remembered the way he had been looking. "No," I said. "I think he was feeling bad. He said he was feeling a little nauseous. His mother didn't want him to play. But he did anyway. He said it was nothing."

"Did he say he had any pain?"

"No. But during the game he was holding his side."

He turned to the other doctor. "Almost certainly the liver. Internal bleeding. Given his skin color, there's a good chance there was already a problem. If his liver was already compromised, a sudden impact could have caused the liver to fail. Let's get him stabilized and run some tests. Right away. There's no time to fool around."

"What's his name?" the doctor asked me, again talking like this was all matter of fact.

"Kurt," I said.

The doctor bent over the patient, shined a tiny light in his eyes. "Kurt, can you hear me?"

"No response," said the other doctor. "Let's get him upstairs."

chapter five

The door opened and the nurse from the front desk came in with Kurt's parents. Both of them were visibly shaken when they saw Kurt passed out on the bed. His mother picked up his hand and seemed shocked by the feel of it. It was cold and clammy. I knew because I had held his hand during the ambulance ride. It was scary.

Kurt's father started to talk to the doctors in a shaky, almost angry voice. "Do what you have to do." Then he looked at them suspiciously. "Are you guys the best available?" he continued. "I only want the best for my son."

"Look," the young doctor said. "We have to get him upstairs right away. We think there's damage to the liver. No time to waste. Will you go out front and fill out the permission form?"

They began to wheel Kurt out of the room. The nurse pulled Kurt's mother's hand away from her son, and Kurt's mom turned and saw me for the first time.

"What's she doing here?" she screamed hysterically, glaring at me as if I was some-how responsible for this.

I tried to say something, but my voice still wasn't working right. I ignored Mrs. Richards and tried to follow Kurt to the elevator. I was grabbed by an orderly and pulled back. He led me away from Kurt's parents toward a small waiting room.

Right then I didn't trust anyone. That expression on Kurt's mother's face was still burning a hole right through me. I wrenched free of the orderly and ran for the front door. Outside, I kept on running until I was six blocks away and my eyes were so filled with tears that I couldn't see enough to keep going.

When I phoned the hospital later, the switchboard lady said that I couldn't be connected to Kurt's room.

"Well, then let me speak to the doctor," I insisted.

"Your name please?" she asked.

"Tina Wright."

"You're not a member of the immediate family?"

I didn't get it. Why was she putting me off? "I'm his friend, okay?" I snapped.

"Sorry, I can't help you. Only immediate family can talk to the patient's doctor," she said and the line went dead.

It drove me crazy all night, not knowing if Kurt was going to be okay. I kept thinking about all the good times we'd had together. I couldn't believe that things might never be the same again. Kurt was the only guy I had ever known who treated me like I really mattered. I had other friends, but none like Kurt. He was different.

I kept thinking about when my parents had been fighting and I was so upset I couldn't think straight at school. It seemed like everybody in town knew about the loud screeching battles between my mom and dad. It was hard to live with everyone knowing about it. Kurt used to sit in the cafeteria with me sometimes, through lunch, and right into the afternoon. One day, he stayed there with me after Mr. Findlay told us to go to class. Even after Mr. Findlay gave us both three days detention, Kurt kept his cool because he knew how upset I was. Then he walked over to Findlay, said something to him, and Findlay left. Kurt sat back down and stayed with me until I was human again. That's the kind of friend he was.

After school that day we didn't go to detention, even though we both knew we would be in big trouble. Instead Kurt took me to Point Pleasant Park and we hiked up to a place he called the Ledge. We sat there on a rock overlooking the Northwest Arm.

We talked and watched the setting sun. After that I knew I could handle the crap my parents were throwing around.

chapter six

Finally, at about three o'clock in the morning, I gave up trying to fall asleep. I got dressed and sneaked out of the house.

There was no bus, so I had to walk the two miles to the hospital. I ran part of the way. It was really weird going through Halifax alone in the middle of the night.

A couple of cars went by and one lady even stopped to ask me if I was okay. "You need a ride somewhere or something?"

I wasn't sure what to do, but I said no. "I'm fine," I said.

"Are you sure? It's awful late. Maybe you should get in."

She was probably trying to help, but I was feeling scared. I didn't trust anyone, especially a stranger. So I ran. It was a good thing that I had been practicing with Kurt. I had good lungs and strong leg muscles.

I knew they weren't going to welcome me at the hospital. I tried to calm myself down, but I know I looked frazzled when I reached the front desk.

"I need to see my brother, Kurt Richards," I lied to the nurse. "He had an accident and he's here somewhere."

She checked through some lists. "He's in intensive care. You can't go in."

"But there must be something somebody can tell me," I pleaded.

She could see I was desperate. "There's a waiting room on the third floor. A doctor will be around."

"Thanks," I said and ran for the elevator. When the door opened, I saw Kurt's

29

parents huddled together on a vinyl sofa. I didn't care what they thought of me.

"How is he?" I asked.

Mrs. Richards looked up at me and said, "Leave us alone. You have no business here. He's our son." She turned away but then looked back at me. "What are you doing here, anyway? Where are your parents? Do they even know you're here?"

I stood my ground, still trying to figure out what I had done to get this lady so down on me. It was so stupid. She thought I was a bad influence on her son just because my parents fought sometimes. It wasn't like their family didn't have a few problems too.

Kurt's father patted her on the shoulder and got up. He walked me to the other side of the room and whispered, "Now's the time Kurt needs just his family. You shouldn't be here." He was trying to sound cool and unemotional.

"Yeah, but I am."

He sighed. "Okay. Here's what we know. There's some sort of damage to ... one of his organs ... his liver."

I think I squinched up my face thinking about it. But I swallowed hard and tried to look serious.

"It's not functioning properly. He'd been to the doctor with a liver problem before and was treated. But the problem must have come back and we didn't realize it. When he got kicked in the game, it made things... well, a lot worse." Mr. Richards rubbed his hand across his face.

"How much worse?" I asked.

"We're not sure. Everything is under control."

"Is he going to live?"

Suddenly Mr. Richards seemed angry with me for asking. "Live? Tina, everything is going to be all right. This is just... one of those things... it's not a life or death situation. Kurt will be fine. It's all under control."

I looked him straight in the eyes, but he turned back to his wife. "Now go on home. We don't need you here, and you're upsetting my wife."

I saw a doctor walking our way. He had a clipboard.

"Can you tell me how Kurt Richards is doing?" I asked him. I wanted to hear the news straight from the doctor, not just from Kurt's dad.

He looked at his clipboard then up at me. "Who are you?"

"His friend," I said. Why didn't I have a right to know something?

But already two hands had grabbed me by the shoulders and pulled me roughly aside. Kurt's father pointed a finger toward the elevator, and I backed away.

"Any news?" he asked the doctor.

"He's stable for now," the doctor said.

"Good," said his father. "Then everything is going to be okay." He said it like it was all over and life was going to shift back to normal.

Somehow I knew better. I had a feeling that Kurt's father was trying to convince himself and his wife that there was no further danger. And that wasn't what I had seen in the doctor's eyes.

Still, I couldn't stand another confrontation. I slipped onto the elevator and left.

chapter seven

Six days went by, and no one would tell me a thing. Kurt's parents hung up when I called. I tried getting up to the third floor in the hospital again, but each time I tried someone told me that since I wasn't family I wasn't allowed.

Nobody at school knew anything. The story going around was that Kurt was getting better and he just had to stay in the hospital for "a while." It was one of the hardest weeks of my life. I flunked every test that came my way and couldn't read three lines in a book without forgetting what I had just read.

Then I was at my locker after fifth period and who shows up but Jason, chewing bubble gum. "So, are you going to be there for the unveiling of the new improved Kurt Richards today?" he asked. Then he blew a pink bubble in my face.

"What are you talking about?"

Jason sucked the gum back in and it caught on his cheek. He tried to untangle it from the puny growth of hair on his top lip. "We're invited to visit the fallen hero," he said sarcastically, "the living legend of the soccer field who didn't even last one game into the season."

I could have slapped the smirk off his face. "Who invited you?"

"His mom."

It figures, I thought. Leave it to her to invite a dork like Jason and not me. But it sounded like good news to me anyway. It meant Kurt was improving. I heaved a sigh of relief.

"What time?" I asked.

"Three-thirty."

"What room?"

Jason took out a slip of paper and read the number. "Three fifty-seven." Then he popped his gum into the slip of paper, wadded it up and batted it with the palm of his hand across the hallway. "Should be good for a laugh," he said.

I slammed the locker in his face and walked away. I should have been mad at the jerk, but all I could think about was going to see Kurt. I would be there, invited or not. My heart jumped up in my throat.

I got to the waiting room at three-thirty and, this time, no one stopped me. When I walked off the elevator I heard the snickering first; then I saw Wicket, Jason, Dorfman and Leach—all guys from the team. None of them were really good friends of Kurt's. Kurt was a loner like me. That was why we had always understood each other so well.

"Hi Tina," Wicket said, trying to be polite.

"Thought you weren't invited," Jason teased. He knew there was tension between Kurt's folks and me. I said nothing. Jason was hugging his motorcycle helmet like he'd been doing all week at school. He had just got his license and his parents had bought him a spanking new Kawasaki. Carrying around the helmet was his way of gloating over his new toy in front everyone—Kurt included, I suppose.

The door to room 357 opened and Kurt's father walked out. "Thanks for coming, guys." I hid behind Wicket. "Come on in. Kurt's anxious to see you."

I slinked in last and stood near the back of the room, avoiding Kurt's father. Mrs. Richards wasn't around, thank God.

Then I saw him, propped up in bed. I almost didn't recognize him. His face looked sort of yellow and his eyes were sunken in. He had a tube going up his nose and another going into his arm. Everything was secured with white tape and the tubes were hooked up to dripping bottles. Kurt tried to smile but had a hard time faking that he was happy to see everybody.

Nobody said anything and then Jason pointed to another clear plastic sack that was suspended from a hanger at the bottom of the bed. It was connected to a tube that came from under the covers on the bed.

"How's it going, dude?" Dorfman asked.

Kurt coughed and cleared his throat. "No homework. No responsibilities. It's like a vacation," he said. There was little energy in his voice.

Kurt hadn't seen me yet. I was still hiding. If Mr. Richards was going to throw me out, I wanted to be able to hang around as long as I could before he did.

"Did we win?" Kurt asked. Everybody knew what he meant.

"Nah," Jason answered. "We lost by one goal. If you'd made your shot it would have been a tie." Good old Jason wanted to rub it in, even now.

"Easy, dude," Dorfman said, putting an elbow in Jason's ribs, then turning to Kurt he asked, "When you getting out?"

Kurt shrugged. His father interjected, "We don't know for sure when he can leave. His liver has been badly damaged. He's still bleeding inside."

"Gross," Leach responded.

"Tough break," Jason said. "Hard to stay in shape when you're in a hospital bed." He flexed his muscles like he was trying to make the most of it. Dorfman smacked him on the side of the head.

"How's school?" Kurt asked, sounding like he was half interested, half asleep. Maybe it was the drugs. He might have been on painkillers.

Nobody knew what to say. They shuffled their feet and stared down at the floor. The room grew quiet—too quiet. The silence was broken by the sound of liquid dripping down a tube and emptying into a plastic bag. Jason nodded toward it to draw everyone's attention. Kurt didn't notice. I think he was fading off to sleep.

We all looked at the tube coming out from under the sheet. It was clear and the fluid inside it was a sickly yellow with streaks of red.

"I think I'm going to be sick," Leach said and looked around the room for a good place to puke. All he found was a trashcan.

He threw himself over it and heaved out his lunch.

Wicket and Dorfman looked like they were about to do the same. They held their noses and ran for the door. Leach followed, his head hung over in embarrassment. Only Jason and I stood there. Jason had a stupid grin on his face like he thought it was all happening for his personal entertainment. I shoved him toward the door and he took the hint.

I'm not sure if Kurt knew what had freaked out the guys. And I don't know if he knew that I wasn't supposed to be there, but he noticed me for the first time. So did his dad. Mr. Richards was about to speak, but I fired a look at him that would fry meat. He stayed quiet.

I walked to Kurt's side and he held up his hand. I grabbed onto it and gave a squeeze. He squeezed back, but he didn't seem to have much strength. I leaned over and put my cheek next to his. I closed my eyes and realized he was crying when I felt his tears run down my cheek. "Thanks for coming, Tina," he said in a whisper. "Stay with me."

When I opened my eyes, I saw Mr. Richards carry the trashcan full of vomit out of the room. He closed the door quietly behind him.

chapter eight

After that, nobody tried to stop me from visiting Kurt. I still didn't feel comfortable when Kurt's mother was there. I guess she was trying to be nice to me, but she really got on my nerves.

"You're such a loyal friend," she'd say in a haughty voice. But the way she said it sounded like an insult. I wanted to say something to her, but I just kept my mouth shut.

"Kurt's improving nicely," Mr. Richards would say. But that wasn't quite the way I saw it.

When they were out of the room, I'd say to Kurt, "Squeeze my hand. Hard." This was my little test to try and figure out if he really was getting better.

He'd squeeze, but there wasn't much to it. He was still pretty weak. And he seemed depressed.

"I know what you must be feeling," I said to him ten days after he had first arrived in the hospital. I'd said it to him before, but today things were different.

"No you don't," he snapped back. "You don't know what it's like at all."

I felt a little hurt.

"This whole situation stinks. It shouldn't have happened to me." He was really angry.

"No, it shouldn't have," I said. "You'll get better."

"I think it's the hospital. The longer I stay here, the more I think I'll never get out. They just keep me here so they can keep the hospital in business. If I just had a chance to get outside, to go home, I'd get better. I know it."

The door opened and two doctors came in. They were very calm and quiet. They checked the chart on the bed and then one of the monitors beside the bed I recognized Dr. Bennington, the young doctor who had been in Emergency when Kurt had arrived. He'd been a regular, but the other guy was new. Something was up.

While they were in the room, Kurt seemed angrier. The doctors always made him mad. When the door closed behind them, he whispered to me, "They don't know what they're doing. If they did, they'd have me fixed up by now."

"I'll be right back," I said. I decided to talk to Bennington myself. Maybe Kurt's parents knew the whole truth. But I knew Kurt didn't, and I sure as heck didn't have all the facts.

I don't usually sneak up on people and snoop, but Bennington and his buddy were standing at the nursing station desk with their backs to me. No one else was around. Bennington was pointing at Kurt's chart, which was in his hand.

I crept up silent as a cat and ducked behind the nurse's station.

"I estimate that the liver is only working at about twenty-five percent," Bennington said. "He's going to have to stay in treatment for a long while, maybe indefinitely."

The other doctor disagreed. "I don't think that's going to do it. In fact, I think that his confinement here is dragging him down. Look at these other indications. I don't think we're doing enough. Besides, he needs continual transfusions and he's got B-negative blood. Our supplies are running low. Have you been able to use blood from his family?"

"No luck there. I already tested them. We're going to have to put a call out for more blood. But aside from that, what else can we do?" Bennington asked.

"Only one thing to do," the other doctor said. "I don't think we have much choice."

I felt a cold wave of panic come over me.

I didn't really understand what they were saying, but it sounded scary.

"But look at the blood type," Bennington said. "You realize how hard it will be to find a matching donor?"

"Without a transplant, he could die. In fact, I'd say the odds are good that he will die without one. Even if he stays hooked up to everything we can muster and even if we can keep him stocked in fresh blood, he's in very bad shape."

That's when the day nurse rounded the corner and bumped into me. She started to curse, and I straightened myself and said I was sorry. Bennington immediately recognized me and realized I had overheard their discussion.

"What are you doing?" the nurse asked me. "You're not allowed back here. Now get."

I ignored her.

"What do you need to save Kurt?" I asked Dr. Bennington point blank. I wasn't sure I fully understood what they were talking about. Something about a transplant, but I didn't understand the rest.

Bennington took off his glasses. "You don't miss much, do you?"

"No," I said. "Is Kurt gonna die?"

"Not if we can help it. We'll do everything we can. Today I'll put out a call to hospitals all over the East for a possible donor."

"What about me?" I asked, not knowing what I was saying.

Bennington shook his head. "Each of us only has one liver. And you can't live without it. Sorry. The donor has to be dead. The blood type has to be a match and we need permission to harvest the organ."

I felt like everything was collapsing around me.

"But we do need blood," the other doctor said. I think he had seen my despair. "What's your blood type?"

I shrugged.

He pulled a notepad out of his pocket, scratched down something and handed it to me. "Two flights down. They only take a little blood. It doesn't hurt."

I took the paper and headed to the elevator. My head was dizzy. I prayed that I had the right blood type. I'd give as many pints as I could if it helped keep Kurt alive. I turned around, realizing Kurt would wonder why I had not come back.

"Don't worry," Bennington said. "I'll tell your boyfriend you'll be back later."

I decided not to explain that I wasn't Kurt's girlfriend. I just cared for him, that's all. And I wanted him to get better.

chapter nine

I lay there with my eyes closed and prayed that it would come out right, that I would have the right match—B negative, whatever that meant.

After I sat for twenty minutes in a waiting room looking at magazines a nurse returned with a form. "Take this back to Dr. Bennington," she said. The envelope was sealed.

In the elevator, I ripped the envelope open. I couldn't wait. I didn't understand most of it but there it was— "Blood type: O positive." I wouldn't be able to donate my blood to help Kurt. When I found Bennington and handed him the ripped-open envelope, he could tell by the look on my face that I wasn't going to be a blood donor.

"It was a long shot," Bennington said. "B negative or O negative are okay, but nothing else will work. Besides, you're not old enough to give legal consent. It would be up to your parents."

"No it wouldn't," I said. It was my body, not theirs.

Maybe I couldn't give Kurt what he needed. But I was determined to make sure he had enough blood until the stupid system could come up with something to really fix him up. At school the following day, I asked everyone I knew what type of blood they had.

"What are you, some kind of vampire?" Dorfman asked. "Besides, I don't know stuff like that. Hanging around hospital beds is making you weird."

I sloughed it off.

"What do you want to know for?" Leach asked. "It's personal even if I did know."

"I'm doing a project for biology," I lied. "It's a survey, okay?"

But he just walked away.

I got a few answers from girls I knew. They seemed less uptight about it than the guys. A couple of teachers laughed at me but told me what kind of blood they had.

Nobody had the right type.

I guess the doctors were right about one thing: It wasn't going to be easy.

By the end of the day I was feeling beat. Scared too. I was just closing my locker when Jason showed up. He came up so close I could smell his breath, and I knew then that he had been drinking. He had his stupid motorcycle helmet under one arm and a big grin on his face.

Some girls thought he was cute, but I knew the guy was a jerk. Ever since his birthday, he'd been a jerk with a motorcycle, which was twice as bad.

"What do you want?" I asked him.

He ignored my question, as if I should be flattered that he had stopped by to talk. "I hate wearing this thing," he said, handing the helmet to me. "The law has no right to say what's safe for me. It cuts down my vision. Besides, on a bike, you're supposed to feel free."

"Right," I said. "Now buzz off." I'd overheard Jason talking non-stop about his motorcycle all week. Everybody was impressed but me.

"Aren't you gonna ask?"

"Ask what?" I snapped.

"You know. My blood type. The guys think your little game is really weird. Dorfman says you're a vampire."

"Give me a break."

"Does it have something to do with loverboy?"

"No." There was no way he was going to trick me into saying anything about Kurt. "Just a biology project."

"No it isn't," Jason insisted, breathing boozy breath all over me again.

"It's none of your business. Take your helmet and go ride your tricycle off a cliff, okay?" I shoved the helmet at him, but he wouldn't take it.

Instead he pulled a folded piece of notebook paper out of his pocket and dropped it in the helmet.

"Read it," he said. "And tell me if I'm the one you're looking for. I charge twenty dollars a pint. But you have to promise not to leave teeth marks."

Jason started to walk away with that cocky dance that he did. "Take your helmet," I said, walking after him.

"No way. It messes with my freedom and interferes with my style."

I wasn't about to chase after him. I opened my locker and had to squeeze the stupid helmet in with all my books and gym stuff. I wasn't even going to look at the note or play along with his stupid game but as I was slamming the locker shut, the paper fell to the floor. I picked it up and unfolded it.

There was a big goofy drawing of a female vampire that I guessed was supposed to be me. And underneath it was simply: "B negative."

chapter ten

I walked out the front door of the school and saw Jason, on his stupid motorcycle, take the corner where the buses were loading. He was going so fast his tires sprayed stones as he went onto the shoulder. I was going to have to talk to him. He was old enough to consent to giving blood. The decision would be his. Maybe I could use his big-shot-nothing-scares-me attitude to con him into it. I had that working for me.

On the other hand, the guy had a very thick skull. Maybe I wouldn't be able to make him understand.

I could have taken the bus, but I decided to walk home instead. I tried to keep my mind focussed on Kurt, but I was already trying to figure out how to convince Jason to give blood, maybe even on a regular basis if Kurt needed it.

As I walked I thought about how things had already started to change between Kurt and me. It was only recently that soccer seemed to get in the way of our friendship. And that was probably because of Jason. Kurt was always trying to prove something to Jason. Kurt wanted desperately to be Jason's friend, but Jason only made his life difficult. Kurt tried to explain to me that Jason had something to teach him. About soccer. About going beyond what you think you're capable of. About going for broke.

I remembered something else too. I remembered how Kurt and I had become friends. I had come home from school one day a couple of years earlier. My parents were inside screaming at each other. The doors were locked and I wanted to go in but was afraid to.

Kurt walked by and saw me sitting on my porch with my head on my knees. When he walked up to me he heard my parents inside.

"What's going on?" he'd asked.

"Listen. World War Three," I'd said.

"You want to come over to my house? Maybe watch a video or something?"

"What do you have?"

"I have all the old *Star Wars* movies. Do you like *Star Wars*?"

I didn't really like science fiction at all, but it didn't matter. I walked to Kurt's house and we watched the first *Star Wars* movie. He talked through the whole thing, explaining who all the characters were and what he knew about each planet. I didn't like the movie much, but I really liked Kurt trying to explain it all to me. He even put his hand over his mouth, started breathing funny and did an imitation of Darth Vader.

Kurt's mother was nice to me the first day except she felt obliged to tell me about the rules at her house. Shoes off when you come in, so you don't wreck the white carpet. No drinks or junk food in the living room. No interfering with homework time. Yikes, she was pushy. I was surprised Kurt was so casual about it.

After I had shown up unnanounced a couple of times, afraid to go home, she wasn't so friendly. She'd heard stories from the neighbors about my parents' fights. The arguments were legendary in our neighborhood. She didn't want her son spending too much time with a kid from a messed up family.

But that day of the first visit, Kurt even walked me home. We stood at my back door and listened. It was quiet.

"Do you think it's safe?" he asked.

"They only yell. They never hit."

"Call me if you need me," Kurt said.

And sometimes I called. Sometimes his mom lied and said Kurt wasn't home. But Kurt had a call minder on the phone in his room. If he saw that I had called, he called me back. Sometimes I just needed someone to talk to.

And Kurt had always been there.

We rode bikes together and then we started running long distance. Sometimes we kicked a soccer ball around at the park—at least until soccer season. That's when he started to get more serious and began practising with the older guys. And he started hanging around with Jason. I don't know why Jason didn't like me. I don't think it was personal because he could be nasty to just about anyone. It didn't seem to bother Kurt, though.

So I decided to stay on the sidelines at the games and practices. I would be Kurt's number one fan. I'd cheer him on. After all, that's what friends are for.

My parents still had problems, but nothing would change that. I loved them, but I found it hard to be in the same room with both of them at the same time. I tried a few times to talk to my mom about it, but she always pretended that we were perfectly normal. "Everything is fine. All families have...difficulties." I promised myself that when I grew up I'd never be like them. I would find someone I truly loved, and I'd live happily ever after. I really would.

chapter eleven

When I got home the house was empty, as usual. Both my parents worked now. They had crummy jobs and there never seemed to be enough money. So what else was new? At least it was quiet.

In my empty house, I sat down and tried to watch TV. The soaps were on. Peggy just found out that she had been cheated out of her inheritance and she was crying. I switched it off in disgust. What crap! People crying because they were no longer rich. That's just the way everybody was. They cared about garbage. Nobody cared about what was really important.

I was angry at the way things were going. And I was so confused too. There was so much about Kurt's problem that I didn't understand. Bennington made it sound unlikely that they would find a liver for Kurt. "We're doing as much as we can," he had said. "Unless a donor comes forward, there's not much we can do except continue to take good care of Kurt." The big trouble, I knew, was that the liver donor had to be dead first.

Whatever they were doing at the hospital, it wasn't enough. I was angry and I was very tired. I dozed into a fitful sleep on the sofa.

Then the doorbell rang. I shook the sleep off and opened the door.

"Who do you think you are spreading rumors about Kurt's condition around school?" Kurt's mother snapped at me as soon as I opened the door. Behind her Mr. Richards looked upset and uncomfortable.

"What are you talking about?"

"I heard from Mrs. Leach that you were scouting around for blood for transfusions or some such thing. That's none of your business. Ever since I met you, little girl, you've been so pushy. Always trying to influence Kurt... the wrong way."

"Where are your parents?" Mr. Richards interjected, with a shade more cool in his voice.

"They're not here," I said. "And you're wrong. I'm trying to help."

"You're just a kid!" Kurt's father shouted at me. "We've got doctors there, some of the best trained men in the country." He said the word *men* like that was what counted. Men could handle these things. Not women. And especially not girls.

"If we don't do everything we possibly can, Kurt could die!" I screamed at them.

"Who told you that?" Mrs. Richards screamed back. "Who told you that? It's not true." She leaned back against her husband and started to cry.

Mr. Richards looked at me and, almost whispering, said, "How did you know?"

"I overheard it. I was there when the specialist came. I know that it's not just the rare blood type. He needs a transplant too. It's true, isn't it?"

Mrs. Richards was lost in her tears. For a brief flash it was all too weird to be real. I thought I had fallen asleep in the middle of a soap opera and was dreaming.

But Mr. Richards nodded his head without speaking. I knew then that it was all too real.

"We don't know what we're going to do," he said, choking back his own tears.

The phone rang. I looked at it just so that I didn't have to look at them. But I let it ring nine times before I moved to answer it.

"Hello?"

"Tina. It's Dr. Bennington at the hospital. Do you know where Kurt is? Is he with you?"

"I don't understand. No, of course he's not here."

"He's not in his room. He's just...well— he's gone. I tried his parents' house, but there was no answer. We had your name and address from the blood clinic. I thought maybe you had concocted some scheme with Kurt..."

I cut him off. "I didn't concoct some scheme," I told him. But I thought about what Kurt had said the other day. He said he felt it was the hospital that was keeping him down, that if he left, he'd get better. I thought maybe he was trying to prove something to himself. "What will happen to him without...without all the tubes and stuff?" I didn't have the right words, but I knew that without the bottles and the equipment, he could be in trouble.

"I don't know. He might pass out, go into shock. He might die."

I slammed down the phone. Kurt's parents knew immediately what had happened. "He said yesterday that he had to get out of the hospital," Mr. Richards said. "It was driving him crazy. I didn't think he'd do it like this."

Mrs. Richards said nothing. She didn't have to. Her expression said it for her: *It's all your fault, Tina.*

chapter twelve

Mr. Richards drove like a maniac to the hospital. I insisted on going with them. Kurt's mother couldn't stop me. She lectured me all the way to the hospital about what a bad influence I'd been on her son and how he used to be such a good boy.

"Nothing like this ever happened to us before," she whimpered.

Mr. Richards had just gone through a red light and had come within inches of picking off two little old ladies with shopping bags. He swerved to avoid them, then squealed the tires as he raced on toward the hospital.

"Kurt was never like this!" she went on. "He always did as he was told. He was a good boy. Nothing bad ever happened to him."

I could see that Kurt's father was as fed up with her complaining as I was. I should have just kept my mouth shut, but I couldn't.

"Would you just stop feeling sorry for yourself and think about your son!" I shouted at her. "All I ever did to Kurt was suggest he'd be better off if he thought for himself and stopped accepting your rules all the time." There, I'd said it. That's the sort of bad influence I was.

She turned around and gave me an icy stare. "And if he wasn't always trying to *think for himself*, he might still be in the hospital bed and not out in the street somewhere."

Mr. Richards slowed down to make the turn into the hospital parking lot. I'd taken all I could stand. I threw open the door and jumped out just as he made the turn. I landed on the grass, rolled once and got up running. Let them do what they could to find Kurt. I know him better than anyone, I thought, and I'll know where to find him.

It felt good to be running. I knew that every minute counted. It was like my legs already knew which direction to go. I was afraid to stop, but I asked myself, *why south? Why this way?* I was headed down Tower Road. *Why would he go this way?*

Then my brain told me what my legs already knew. I was running toward Point Pleasant Park. It was the part of the city closest to the ocean. Kurt always said he felt more alive when he was near the sea. We had gone there on our bicycles dozens of times.

Kurt had it in his head that the hospital was the reason he wasn't getting better. And now he thought he needed to get outside, to get to the ocean. I ran until my lungs ached from overwork.

I ran through the big iron gates and down the wide forest path. I passed a cop on a horse and a bunch of rowdy kids my own age who were throwing pine cones at each other. Seeing them made me realize how much things had changed for Kurt and me. They were kids, still goofing off. For me and Kurt, everything was forever different. And if I was wrong with my guess, maybe my whole world was about to collapse.

I went west along a narrow trail. I tripped over roots and rocks, stumbled and banged up my legs, but I kept going. Up ahead was the rock outcropping that looked out over the Northwest Arm of the harbor and on out to sea. It was *our* place.

I thought again about that afternoon we cut detention and Kurt brought me here. I'd never even been to the park before. It was at the end of town where people with money lived. The sun had been going down over the water. It was golden and the pine trees were lit up with the sunlight. He had touched my hand and said, "Let's just be quiet and watch." We looked out over the water for a long while. That's the kind of guy Kurt was.

The trail twisted up the slope, and I had to grab onto the tree roots to keep from sliding down the loose stones. My eyes were having a hard time focussing and my lungs felt ready to explode. Where the trail stopped I heaved myself up onto the rock outcropping, the place we called the Ledge.

I felt his hand as I pulled myself up, even before I could see his face. His hand felt cold. *Kurt!*

He looked like he was just curled up asleep. I bent over him and put my ear to his mouth. My heart was racing so fast, and I was breathing so hard that at first I couldn't tell... I held my breath and waited. I felt his breath on my cheek. He was breathing. He was alive, but he wasn't okay. I rolled him over but couldn't see any bleeding.

I knew that the problem wasn't on the outside. It wasn't anything you could see. His breathing was shallow and jerky. I needed to get him back to the hospital—and fast—but

I couldn't carry him down. It was too steep and too dangerous. I wasn't strong enough and, besides, I could do more harm.

I think that the hardest thing for me to do, just then, was to leave him alone. All I had on was a light jacket and I threw it over him. Then I scrambled down from the Ledge and ran for help.

When I got to the main pathway, I stopped two guys on racing bikes. I asked one of them to phone an ambulance. The other one I asked to search for the cop I'd seen. They could tell from how freaked-out I was that I was serious. They sped off in opposite directions, and I sat down in the dirt to gather my wits.

chapter thirteen

The ambulance arrived and the attendant, Martha, recognized me at once.

"Get in," she said. "You're getting to be a regular customer."

I was shaking and just plain scared. She put a blanket around me and cupped an oxygen mask over Kurt.

"It wasn't my idea," I said. "He should have stayed in the hospital."

She gave me a curious glance. "Nobody said it was, honey. Relax. Boy, you sure have your hands full looking after this guy. You're sure he's worth all the trouble?"

"Yeah, he's worth it," I said. I liked her. I knew that she was teasing me in a gentle way to make things seem less scary. I knew she was someone I could trust. While we talked, the driver was whipping down the street with his siren going.

"Shut that damn thing off," Martha said. "We're almost there. So just can it."

The siren wound down with a mournful howl that faded to nothing.

"Know anything about how a liver works?" I asked her.

She shrugged. "Can't live without it. That his problem?"

"Yeah, I guess he needs a new one or he dies."

"Transplant time?"

"If they find a donor before it's too late."

We backed into the ambulance loading bay and had just come to a stop when another ambulance came roaring in beside us. That driver had the siren up full blast. It was murder on the ears. Two orderlies were about to unload Kurt when the driver of the other ambulance yelled. "This one first. Heart stopped twice. Head injury. Got to get him in quick!"

The orderlies headed to the other ambulance.

I jumped out and started after them. "Wait! We're important too," I said. But Martha had grabbed hold of my shoulders.

"Just be calm. Your boyfriend's more or less stable. That, over there, sounds very bad. Be cool." She adjusted the oxygen mask on Kurt.

I watched as the other stretcher was unloaded. There was blood all over, and I heard the driver say, "Motorcycle accident. The kid drove into a car and flew over the roof. No helmet. It looks bad."

As the cart came past us, a doctor approached to get a look at the head wound. When he pulled back the temporary bandage, I got a look at a long gash on his face.

I almost didn't recognize him at first. It was Jason. The idiot had left his helmet with me. It was still in my locker. They wheeled Jason through the open doors and out of view.

Two other attendants came out and unloaded Kurt. I walked with them as far as the door and then Martha tugged me back again.

"Come on," she said. "I'll buy you a Coke." She had seen my expression when they had wheeled Jason past. She didn't know what the story was, but she knew I needed a friend. I felt like the world had gone hopelessly insane.

In the hospital cafeteria, I explained everything to Martha. She listened well. I didn't touch the Coke. "Jason is a jerk, but now I feel like I was somehow responsible for his accident. I didn't chase after him to give him back his helmet."

"It wasn't your fault. He didn't want to wear it. You said it yourself. He thought he was being cool, I suppose."

"But he didn't deserve this."

"Honey, most people who get hurt don't deserve it."

Then I told Martha about the picture of me as a vampire. "I think, in his own stupid way, Jason was trying to tell me he was willing to donate some of his blood for transfusions. He even had the right blood type. But now Jason's the one who's going to need blood. And there's not a thing I can do to help either of them."

Martha gave me a soft, sad look. "I'm afraid you just have to trust the system."

I know she was just trying to be helpful, but right then, I didn't trust anybody or anything. I walked outside and down the street to a park where I sat on a kid's swing. I swung back and forth, kicking my feet high up in the air. I was remembering what it was like to be a kid. Everything had seemed so simple then. It seemed like only yesterday.

chapter fourteen

"He's awake," Dr. Bennington told me. "You can go in."

Kurt was propped up in bed. This time he didn't have a tube shoved up his nose. It was good to see him smile. I sat down on the edge of the bed, almost afraid to touch him—afraid that if I did, I might injure him in some way.

"I knew you'd know where to find me."

"Yeah. That's our place."

"Except it wasn't supposed to be like that. I'm sorry."

I shrugged. "You made a mistake, you big goof. Why'd you leave like that?"

Kurt held out his hand and I took it. For once it felt almost normal. "I didn't believe all they were telling me. Laying around all day was making me feel lousy. I figured if I could just get out of here—even for a little while—I'd feel better."

"I know," I said. "Have they told you everything?" I asked.

"God, I hope so. All they say is that I am to stay hooked up to all of this and stay here until a better option comes along."

"A transplant?" I wanted to be sure he knew.

"Yeah, a transplant. Like in the Frankenstein movies." He looked tired again and real bummed out.

"I always kind of liked Frankenstein," I told him. "He was my hero for a while. A very misunderstood character."

Kurt tried a brave smile. His energy was fading. "Tina, when I woke up and they told me you had tracked me down, I got thinking. I can't believe I've put you through all this. I think you better just leave me alone for a while and see what happens."

"Oh sure," I said. I was angry he was even saying this. It was just like Kurt to try to tough things out on his own.

"No. Really. I'm not much fun like, well, like this." He pointed down to the wires and tubes going under the sheets. "It's been rough on you and it's my fault. So just forget about me until it's all over one way or the other."

This made me so angry I almost smacked him in the face. I took a deep breath instead. "Right," I said with a smirk on my face. "Give up a chance to hang out with Frankenstein? No way." I did something just then that shocked him. I kissed him on the cheek for the first time ever. And then I got up to go.

I should have kept my mouth shut, but I thought Kurt should know. "Kurt, Jason got himself messed up on his new motorcycle. He's downstairs."

Kurt leaned up in bed. "How is he?"

"I don't know," I told him. "I don't know."

"There goes the season," Kurt said. What a weird thing, I thought, to think about soccer after all this. But then Kurt hadn't seen what I had seen.

"Coach will be really ticked off," I said, backing off from saying what I really thought. "I hope Jason is all right."

As I walked out the door, I had to pass Kurt's parents. Mrs. Richards grabbed my sleeve. "You had it all planned, didn't you?"

"What are you talking about?" I closed the door solidly behind me. I didn't want Kurt to hear.

"You could have killed him with your little rendezvous," she said.

"It wasn't my idea," I pulled away and walked on. I didn't need to take any of their crap.

Mr. Richards stalked behind me. "I've talked with the administration. This time, they assure me, you won't be allowed back in the hospital. I've explained the problem to them."

I stopped and spun around. How could they have it all so wrong? I didn't even know where to begin. So I said nothing and walked onto the elevator.

chapter fifteen

A security guy in his early twenties, who looked like a bouncer in a nightclub, escorted me out of the hospital. "Sorry, kid," he said. "It's just my job. I don't usually have to hassle girls. Just stay away, okay? You must've done something to make them unhappy." I felt like a criminal.

Martha was sitting in the lobby. She saw me being ushered outside and followed.

"Leave the kid alone, Muscle Breath," she told the guy.

"She's out of here," he said. "I'm done. Good-bye." And he disappeared back into the hospital.

"What's up?" Martha asked. "My shift was over so I thought I'd hang around."

"Oh, God," I said, trying to hold back the tears. "First Kurt. Now Jason."

"Need a ride?"

"No, I don't know where to go. I sure don't feel like going home."

"Well, what do you feel like?" She was trying to be nice.

I wasn't thinking about Kurt right then. I was thinking about Jason. I'd seen him on the stretcher. It looked bad. "I feel like a vampire," I told her.

"I don't get it."

"I asked everybody I knew what their blood type was. Kurt is B negative. They said he was going to need lots of blood for transfusions. Guess who was the only person I found with the right blood type?"

"Jason?"

"Yeah. And what I think Jason was trying to tell me before the accident, in his own weird way, was that he wanted to help. He really did care about Kurt and was willing to donate his blood." What I was thinking just then was scary and awful enough that I felt ashamed.

Martha said it out loud for me. "And if he dies, you've got yourself an organ donor."

I couldn't look at her. A flood of tears came out of me and I hung onto her shoulder, sobbing.

"Tina, whether Jason lives or dies has nothing to do with you. And whatever we think right now will make no difference to Jason's chances."

"I guess I know that. And I don't really want him to die. It's just that this may be Kurt's only opportunity. Especially now. I think that maybe he's worse off since he ran away from the hospital. More damage."

"I'm gonna see what I can find out about Jason," Martha said. "Stay here."

The minutes dragged on while I waited.

Martha returned as promised. "Severe head injury," she said, looking first at her hands and then down at the floor. "If he'd worn his helmet, he might have been okay, but it's very bad. He's on life support, the sort they use for patients that are what they call 'brain dead.' If his parents agree, they'll pull the plug in eight hours. Absolutely nothing they can do."

I closed my eyes and found that already I missed Jason. I missed his obnoxious macho jokes and his stupid antagonism. I thought about how he and Kurt had grown up in the same neighborhood. Their parents were old chums, and the two kids had often been thrown together. Kurt had always called Jason a friend, though I'd never seen Jason do anything to deserve the title. Jason made fun of Kurt and tried to break him down whenever he could. Guys were funny that way.

Suddenly, I saw something that made me suck in my breath and cover my face with my hands.

We were standing near the glass doors.

Outside, a car skidded to a stop. I knew who was inside. I'd met them before. Jason's father and mother got out and ran past us. I'll never forget the panic in their faces.

Martha understood before I said anything.

"What will happen?" I said. "I feel so helpless."

Martha put her arm around me and began walking me out the doors of the hospital. "You go home. I'll tell Bennington what you told me about the blood type. When the time is right, he'll talk to Jason's parents about a transplant. That's all we *can* do. Now go home." She gave me a gentle push.

But I didn't go home right away. I ran again, all the way back to the Ledge. I watched the sun set over the water. It had a sad beautiful quality that made me think of Jason and Kurt and how stupid life was. When it started to get cold I went home, but I got up at dawn and left a note for my mom. Then I ran all the way back to the hospital.

The morning was gray and cold. The sky was full of bad news, and I kept hoping it was all a dream. It wasn't.

I got as far as the waiting room in the Outpatient Clinic before someone came up from behind me and grabbed my arm.

"This way." The voice was not unfriendly. It was Martha.

"What are you doing here?" I asked.

"You need a friend, Tina. I'm all you've got. And they were serious about keeping you out. By the way, you look like hell."

"Thanks for the news," I said. I let her lead me outside to the ambulance loading bay.

"Get in," she said when we got to her ambulance.

"Why?"

"Just do it."

I got inside and she told me to lie down on the gurney. "I'll take you up to see Bennington."

I lay down and covered myself with a sheet. Martha opened the back door and wheeled me out onto the ramp and back inside the hospital.

"I'm not supposed to be doing this," she told me. She sounded nervous.

We traveled up in a crowded elevator, and I pretended to be unconscious. When she wheeled me off on the fourth floor, she asked a nurse where Dr. Bennington was.

"He's in his office," the nurse said, looking through the glass door. "Don't knock. Just go in."

When we got there, I pulled off the sheet, jumped up and went in through the door, closing it loudly behind me.

Bennington was startled. He looked up from a pile of papers on his desk. "How did you get in here?" he asked, more annoyed than angry.

I shrugged. "How is he?"

"The same," Bennington said. "We're doing everything we can. You know that."

"Did you talk to Jason Evans' parents?"

Bennington seemed surprised. He rubbed his hand along the desk. "Yeah, I just talked to them about half an hour ago." I waited for him to say more, but he sat silently with his fingers locked together in front of him.

"Jason told me his blood is B negative."

"He wasn't lying. It's a perfect match."

"Is Jason alive?"

"The family has decided to discontinue the life support."

I closed my eyes and thought about Jason.

Bennington knew what I wanted to ask next, and he knew it would be hard for me to ask. I didn't have to. "I'm not really supposed to be discussing this with you," he said.

But I just stood there, staring at him. "Please," I begged.

He let out a sigh. "They refused," he said. "It's their right. They've suffered a big blow. That's hard enough and they can't face a decision like this."

"But they can't do that!" I said. "If Jason is going to die and Kurt has a chance to live, then he deserves that chance."

"That's not for us to decide."

"Can I talk to them?"

He snapped immediately. "Absolutely not." He turned cold and professional again. "You leave them alone."

87

"Sure." I was afraid he'd call somebody and have me thrown out. And I didn't want to be thrown out, not while there was still hope.

"We've got calls in to over thirty donor hospitals. Something will come up."

"Right," I said. I didn't believe a word of it. Finding a donor with B-negative blood was nearly impossible. Nothing had come up so far. The odds were stacked against it.

"We're doing all we can. You just have to trust us."

"Sure," I said again.

"Go home and get some rest. You can call me if you like and I'll have the nurses keep you posted on Kurt's condition. But you know Kurt's parents don't want you here. We've been through all that."

Bennington picked up the phone. I knew he was calling for security to escort me out.

"I can find my own way," I said.

chapter sixteen

I took the stairs down to the third floor. As I passed Kurt's room I looked in. Both of his parents were there. His mother was crying and his father was pacing back and forth. Kurt was unconscious. As I pushed up against the glass of the door to get a better look, I could see his skin was an awful yellowish, greenish color. I knew that was because his liver wasn't working. He was getting worse and time was running out.

I felt frozen, totally helpless. I didn't think I could move away from that spot. But someone was walking at a fast clip toward me. I didn't turn around to look. It was Martha again. She gave me a pat on the shoulder. "I know," she said. "I know. Now let's move before those goons behind me start hassling you again."

The "goons" weren't all that scary looking—just two white-coated attendants. But I moved anyway.

We walked toward the elevator and stepped inside. As the door closed Martha waved goodbye to the attendants who had followed us. As we began to go down, she punched the red stop button and we came to a halt between floors.

"What did Jason's parents say?"

"They said no. I have to talk to them," I told her. "I have to convince them." Even as I said it, I didn't know if I had the courage to face them. I was scared to death that I wouldn't say the right words, that I would screw it up somehow and it would be all over. "But I don't know if I can do it."

Martha took my hand and squeezed. She looked me straight in the eye. She punched the second floor button and the elevator started moving

The doors parted. Martha held them open and pointed to the third door down the hall. "They're in there. Wait until there's no doctor or nurse around."

There was nothing in the world that could have stopped me from trying.

My legs seemed to move on their own. I walked down the hall and knocked gently on the door frame. Then I went in.

Jason's head was almost completely bandaged. There were electronic machines beeping and ticking. Jason's parents appeared to be praying. They looked up when I entered.

I had met Jason's parents only twice before. They were wealthy like Kurt's folks and lived in a big house. They had lots of money, but you could tell by the way they dressed they were old-fashioned. They spoiled Jason by giving him anything he wanted, though. That's why he had the motorcycle. They were probably blaming themselves for Jason's accident. I don't know if they had ever thought much about me, but they knew I was Kurt's friend. I knew that Kurt's parents had let on how unhappy they were that Kurt was hanging out with me.

"I'm here to talk about Kurt," I said, looking straight at Jason, not them.

"How dare you!" Jason's father shouted at me.

I pretended I didn't hear. I looked at Jason's mother and spoke in a calm slow voice, hoping the words would do some sort of magic all on their own.

"Jason is probably going to die and it's not going to mean much," I began. "A stupid accident."

"You get out of here right this instant!" Jason's father shouted. I didn't listen.

"It's not fair," I said, "that he has to die. I'll miss him very much, although it's nothing like what you will feel, I know."

Jason's father started for the door. He was going to get someone to throw me out.

I almost panicked and started crying, but Jason's mother pulled him back. "Let's hear what she has to say," she said in a voice full of sadness.

"Jason and Kurt were friends," I said.

"They still *are* friends," Jason's father insisted. "They were always very close. They grew up together."

I could see then that he must not have known what Jason was like to his "friends." And I could tell that he wasn't ready to admit that his son was dying.

"We know that Jason isn't going to make it," Mrs. Evans said. Jason's father just shook his head. He looked angry—like he wanted to hit somebody. He scared me, but I wasn't ready to back off.

"And when he dies," I told her, "he can save Kurt's life. If you give your permission for the transplant."

"We already said no to the doctors. It's too much for us to think about. Too much to ask at a time like this!" Mr. Evans shouted. His hands were clenched into fists and he was right over top of me now. I was sure he was ready to hit me, or hit something, because he was so frustrated and angry that he couldn't do anything for his son.

I held my ground. "It *is* too much to ask," I told him. "And I'm not supposed to be here asking it. But I'm asking it anyway. Jason's death will be worth something because he'll save another life."

He was shaking his head no. Mrs. Evans was sobbing, but I could see she was trying to get control of herself. I was shaking too. I was so scared. I almost wished Mr. Evans *would* hit me and get the anger out of him. Right then I knew I was losing it, and I wanted to feel the pain that Kurt and Jason must have felt.

"Get out!" he said.

"No," I answered. "I'm sorry to do this, but I have to. I think I know how you feel. And maybe you've never thought about donating part of your son's body if he dies. But you have to think about it now. Jason was a tough guy and he didn't back down from much. I think he'd be mad at you if you let him back down from this."

I was shocked that I had come out and said that. I was sure it was the wrong thing to say. But suddenly Jason's mother looked up at me. "You really did know Jason, didn't you?"

"Not all that well," I admitted.

"He just pretended he was tough," his mother said. "Underneath, he was just a little boy trying to act tough."

"I think I knew that."

"He wanted to be the best at everything he did," his father said. "Jason pushed himself hard. He always wanted to be the best he could be, and I think he wanted others to follow his lead."

I nodded in agreement.

He didn't seem so angry now. "I think Jason wanted to be some kind of hero."

I swallowed hard and went for it. "I think he finally has his chance."

The door opened and three doctors walked in. "It's time," one of them said. "You can stay in the room if you like." They had come to shut off the life-support system.

I turned to leave. It had all been in vain.

"Wait," Mr. Evans said. I turned around, but he wasn't talking to me. "We want to see Dr. Bennington," he said.

chapter seventeen

I didn't cry at Jason's funeral, though I was surrounded by all kinds of people in tears, including Leach and Dorfman.

My parents said they'd take time to come with me, but I convinced them it wasn't necessary. So I went by myself. Jason's mom spotted me after the service. She gripped hard onto my hand and wouldn't let go as all the other adults came by to say how sorry they were. I felt confused, but I stood there until she was ready to let go. She never said one word to me.

Mr. Richards came up to me afterwards and said, "We'll give you a ride home." His voice sounded soft and kind.

"Okay."

In the car, they said they wanted me to visit Kurt. He was recovering, they said, but was acting quite strange. They told me I shouldn't be upset by anything he said.

"The poison is still in his system from when his liver wasn't working right. They say it'll take a while to straighten out."

The next time I arrived at the hospital, nobody tried to keep me out. I walked with Kurt's parents through the front door and up to that familiar room.

Kurt was propped up in bed and, it was true, he didn't look good. His parents stayed outside and left the door closed.

"You all right?" I asked.

"Do I look all right?" he snapped.

"You look alive," I said. "That's a start." But he had already hurt my feelings.

"Are you angry at me?" I asked tentatively.

He clenched a fist. He was angry with someone. "No. I don't mean to be. I'm just having a hard time. I keep seeing images of Jason smashing up his bike. And I keep thinking about what a jerk the guy always was. And now part of him is in me and he...you two saved my life." Kurt looked like he was about to scream. "And it's all just so confusing. I don't understand it. And I feel like hitting something."

"I think it's part of the process. I don't know why. You'll feel better eventually."

"Yeah, so they say." Kurt tried to replace the anger with something else. He smiled, then looked worried. "What if I'm not the same anymore? Are you still gonna like me?"

"Don't be silly. Of course I'll *like* you." Leave it to Kurt to use the word *like* at a time like this. It made me feel that he was more back to normal than he thought. "Besides, I don't care if you are different. I think we're all different now."

"I wish things could go back to the way

they used to be. And I wish Jason was still alive."

"We all wish that," I said.

"You never gave up on me, did you? Not even when they tried to keep you away."

"I did what I had to do."

"You're pretty amazing, you know."

I think it was the first time anyone had ever said that to me. I didn't know what to say, so I just looked away. Then he took my hand and held it in his. We both said nothing after that. When I turned my head and looked at him he had this big goofy grin on his face. And I laughed out loud.

chapter eighteen

A few weeks later, when Kurt was finally allowed to go back to school, I watched people trying to be nice to him—too nice. Nobody slapped him on the back. The guys all acted like they were talking to a little old lady when they saw him. Kurt had lost weight and he still looked, well, sick. But he was improving.

Everyone avoided talking about Jason when Kurt was around. Then one day at lunch Dorfman asked, "What's it feel like to be walking around with a piece of old Jason inside you keeping you alive?"

I think until then Kurt had been treating himself like he was a piece of china about to break. Finally somebody had come out and asked him an honest question.

Kurt took a big bite of his sandwich, chewed with a very serious look on his face and swallowed. The table had gone silent. The guys were waiting to see if Kurt was going to crack. Instead he lit into a smile.

"It feels good," he said. "Real good. And now I know what Jason meant about not wimping out when the going gets tough." The guys thought Kurt was talking about Jason, but he was sitting across the table, looking straight at me. I knew what he was getting at, even if they didn't.

"You gonna be able to play soccer again next year?" Leach asked.

"I don't know," Kurt said. "I'll have to see. But if I do, it'll be like two halfbacks for the price of one, you know what I mean?"

Leach nodded. "Yeah, maybe I do."

Walking home together after school that day, Kurt and I saw a young pigeon fly into the side of a moving car. The car kept going, but the pigeon fell into the street.

We ran over to it and Kurt picked it up.

"One of its wings is broken," I said. "Too bad. It's just a young one too."

The driver saw us run onto the street in his rear-view mirror, so he backed up. He looked at the bird in Kurt's hands. "Ah, too bad for the little thing. The stupid bird flew right into the side of my car. There was nothing I could do."

"The wing's busted," Kurt said.

"I can see. Look, kid, the best thing to do when a wild animal gets hurt like that is to just put it in the bushes and let it die."

Kurt looked at the guy and said, "Right. Thanks for the advice."

The driver put his car in gear. He leaned out the window. "Look, I'm sorry, but these things happen all the time." And then he drove off.

"What do you think?" I asked Kurt.

"I think the guy's full of it," Kurt said. "I think I know a vet who'd be willing to try to put a splint on the wing. And I'll take care of it until it heals."

"Right," I said. "Then maybe you and I can teach it to fly all over again."

Lesley Choyce is the author of over fifty books for children, young adults and adults, including two books in the Orca Soundings Series, *Refuge Cove*, and *Thunderbowl*. Lesley lives, surfs and performs spoken word in Nova Scotia.

If you would like further
information about organ donation
or becoming an organ donor,
please check the following websites:

www.organdonor.gov
www.shareyourlife.org
www.hc-sc.gc.ca/english/organandtissue
www.givelife.ca

New
Orca Currents Novel

Wired by Sigmund Brouwer

I cut left to miss a boulder sticking out of the snow. I ducked beneath a branch. I hit a jump at freeway speed. It launched me into the air at least one story off the ground. I leaned forward and made sure my skis stayed straight.

I thumped back to earth and crouched low, so I would block less wind. At this speed, the trees on each side of the slope seemed like flashing fence boards.

Halfway down the run I knew I was skiing the best I ever had. If I kept pushing, I would easily stay at number one.

Beneath my helmet, I grinned my grin of fear. And as I cut into a steep turn, I saw it. But couldn't believe it.

Wire. Black wire stretched between two trees at waist height. I was flashing toward it at thirty meters per second. Hitting the wire at that speed would slice me in two.

New
Orca Currents Novel

Spoiled Rotten by Dayle Campbell Gaetz

I landed heavily on the rough wood of the dock. Somehow I tripped over the rope in my hand and fell sideways. But I never let go of that rope. I scrambled to my feet and eased the boat against the dock.

Dad stepped off to tie the stern rope while I tied the bow. I waited for him to say, "Nice work," or, "Well done," or maybe, "Sorry I yelled at you," but he didn't even look my way. He patted the pockets of his shorts. "Anyone seen my wallet?" he asked.

Amy appeared from nowhere. "I'll get it, Dad," she said and disappeared into the cabin.

I stared after her. Dad? Since when was he her dad? This kid wanted everything that was mine.